Mifflin
Harcourt

PHONICS

Grade 2

ISBN 978-0-544-26775-6

11 12 13 14   0928   22 21 20 19 18

4500702692   A B C D E F G

Core Skills Phonics

Grade 2

Unit 1: Consonants

Unit 2: Vowels

Table of Contents
Core Skills Phonics, Grade 2

Unit 3: Consonant Blends

Unit 4: Consonant Digraphs

Features

The *Core Skills Phonics* series provides skill-specific pages that link phonics with spelling and reading, allowing students to build language skills through integrated activities.

In *Core Skills Phonics*, you will find skill-specific exercises that introduce the sounds of the consonants and vowels.

The **skill box** explains the rule and cites examples.

Exercises allow students to use visual and auditory modalities to explore the skill.

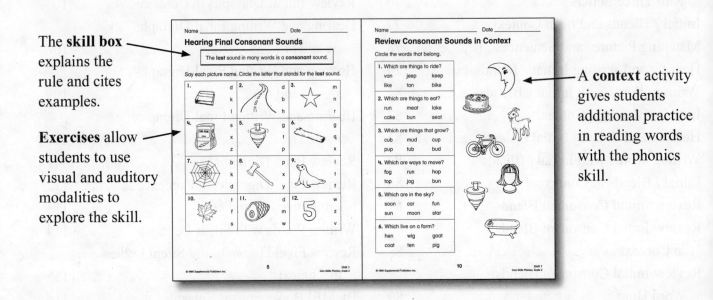

A **context** activity gives students additional practice in reading words with the phonics skill.

Other features include the following:

- unit **reviews** to ensure that students have mastered the skill.

- a **By Me!** book at the end of each unit, which contains phonics-based words, to develop reading comprehension. Students fold the page in half horizontally so that the print shows on both sides. Then they fold it in half again so that the cover faces up.

- **Quiz Yourself!**, an informal test of students' knowledge of the unit skills.

- a **unit assessment** to determine whether students have mastered the phonics skills.

- a **general assessment**, found on pages 1 and 2, which can be used as a diagnostic tool to gauge students' phonics knowledge before instruction or as a final test.

Name _____ Date _____

General Assessment

Name each picture. Circle the letters that stand for the missing blend.
Write the letters to complete the words.

1. st / nd / mp sta__	**2.** sl / sk / sp __unk	**3.** br / bl / tr __ee
4. pl / sp / spl __ant	**5.** scr / cl / spr __ing	**6.** gl / fl / str __ag
7. sw / tw / sn __ins	**8.** sk / cr / nd ha__	**9.** gr / fr / sm __ill
10. squ / spr / spl __are	**11.** sw / dr / squ __ing	**12.** sm / nt / sp wa__

1

Name _____ Date _____

General Assessment, p. 2

Read each sentence. Fill in the circle next to the word that completes the sentence.

I. Take a seat on the park _____.	○ bench ○ wrench ○ bank
2. Shelly _____ a thank-you note.	○ wrote ○ road ○ white
3. The _____ made a big splash in the water.	○ whale ○ wink ○ know
4. When do you think the _____ will hatch?	○ thick ○ shack ○ chick
5. Rice and _____ are good to eat.	○ fence ○ corn ○ cup
6. It is fun to sail a _____ on the lake.	○ bat ○ bone ○ boat
7. Mom will honk the car _____ when she gets there.	○ horn ○ hurt ○ hat
8. A _____ cub does not make a good pet.	○ cot ○ cut ○ cute

General Assessment
Core Skills Phonics, Grade 2

Hearing Initial Consonant Sounds

The letters of the alphabet stand for sounds. The **first** sound in many words is a **consonant** sound.

Say each picture name. Circle the letter that stands for the **first** sound.

1. n m r	**2.** y w z	**3.** t l d
4. y w v	**5.** d b h	**6.** x w y
7. c g qu	**8.** k h b	**9.** s k z
10. s f t	**11.** n r qu	**12.** n k h

Unit 1
Core Skills Phonics, Grade 2

Writing Initial Consonant Sounds

Say each picture name. Write the letter that stands for the **first** sound.

1. _____

2. _____

3. _____

4. _____

5. _____

6. _____

7. _____

8. _____

9. _____

10. _____

11. _____

12. _____

13. _____

14. _____

15. _____

Hearing Final Consonant Sounds

The **last** sound in many words is a **consonant** sound.

Say each picture name. Circle the letter that stands for the **last** sound.

1.	d k l	2.	d b h	3.	m n r
4.	s x z	5.	g t p	6.	g q x
7.	b k d	8.	p x y	9.	l t f
10.	t f s	11.	d m w	12.	w z v

Writing Final Consonant Sounds

Say each picture name. Write the letter that stands for the **last** sound.

1. _____	2. _____	3. _____
4. _____	5. _____	6. _____
7. _____	8. _____	9. _____
10. _____	11. _____	12. _____
13. _____	14. _____	15. _____

Unit 1
Core Skills Phonics, Grade 2

Hearing and Writing Medial Consonant Sounds

> The **middle** sound in many words is a **consonant** sound.

Say each picture name. Write the letter that stands for the **middle** sound.

1.  bea __ __ er	**2.**  ca __ __ in	**3.**  li __ __ ard
4. 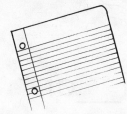 me __ __ al	**5.**  pa __ __ er	**6.**  sa __ __ ad
7. 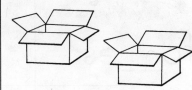 ca __ __ oe	**8.** pa __ __ ade	**9.** bo __ __ es

Unit 1
Core Skills Phonics, Grade 2

Name _____ Date _____

Hearing and Writing Medial Consonant Sounds, p. 2

Say each picture name. Write the letter that stands for the **middle** sound.

1. ca__el	**2.** ba__on	**3.** ro__ot
4. wi__er	**5.** gui__ar	**6.** sho__el
7. fo__es	**8.** ra__or	**9.** spi__er
10. ti__er	**11.** ru__er	**12.** ri__er

8

Review Consonant Sounds

Say each picture name. Write the letters that stand for the **first**, **middle**, and **last** sounds.

1.  __ i __ e __	**2.**  __ a __ a __	**3.**  __ a __ e __
4. 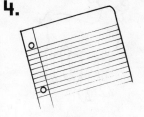 __ a __ e __	**5.**  __ a __ o __	**6.**  __ a __ o __
7.  __ a __ o __	**8.**  __ ea __ e __	**9.**  __ __ o __ e __
10.  __ o __ i __	**11.**  __ o __ a __	**12.**  __ i __ e __

9

Core Skills Phonics, Grade 2

Name _____ Date _____

Review Consonant Sounds in Context

Circle the words that belong.

1. Which are things to ride?

van   jeep   keep

like   tan   bike

2. Which are things to eat?

run   meat   lake

cake   bun   seat

3. Which are things that grow?

cub   mud   cup

pup   tub   bud

4. Which are ways to move?

fog   run   hop

top   jog   bun

5. Which are in the sky?

soon   car   fun

sun   moon   star

6. Which live on a farm?

hen   wig   goat

coat   ten   pig

Unit 1
Core Skills Phonics, Grade 2

Review Consonant Sounds: Riddles

Circle the word that names the picture. Write it on the line.

1. Is it a **fox**, **box**, or an **ox**?  _____

2. Is it a **cap**, **cat**, or **cab**?  _____

3. Is it a **dog**, **hog**, or **log**?  _____

4. Is it a **can**, **pan**, or **van**?  _____

5. Is it a **wig**, **pig**, or **dig**?  _____

6. Is it a **pen**, **pet**, or **peg**? 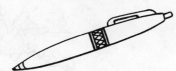 _____

7. Is it a **bug**, **bus**, or **bun**?  _____

8. Is it **men**, **ten**, or a **hen**?   _____

Unit 1
Core Skills Phonics, Grade 2

Reading Comprehension: Consonant Sounds

Circle the sentence that tells about the picture.

1. Rex sees a bug.

Rex sees a tub.

Rex sees a bone.

2. Rex hides.

Rex hops.

Rex eats.

3. Pam gets wet.

Pam gets Rex.

Pam sits.

4. Rex is in a pen.

Rex is dry.

Rex is wet.

5. Rex gets a bed.

Rex gets a prize.

Rex gets a coat.

Name _____ Date _____

Sounds of <u>c</u>

When **c** is before **e**, **i**, or **y**, it can stand for the **s** sound in **sun**. Before other vowels, **c** usually stands for the **k** sound in **kite**.

cent

cat

Name the first picture in each row. Circle the pictures that have the same **c** sound as the first picture.

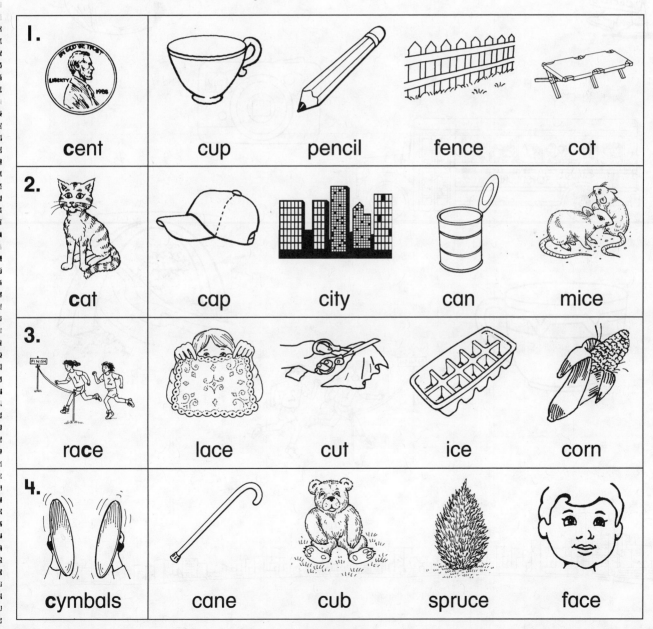

1.				
cent	cup	pencil	fence	cot
2.				
cat	cap	city	can	mice
3.				
ra**c**e	lace	cut	ice	corn
4.				
cymbals	cane	cub	spruce	face

13

Name _____ Date _____

Sounds of c, p. 2

Cecil goes to the city. Color the pictures that have the **c** sound in **city**.

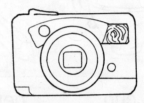

14

Name _____ Date _____

Sounds of c in Context

Read each sentence. Circle the word that completes the sentence.
Write it on the line.

1. Cindy saved ten dollars and fifty _____ . _____	cents cats
2. She wanted to spend it at the _____ . _____	case circus
3. Cindy and Cecil rode in a _____ . _____	cell cab
4. At one tent, they saw some bear _____ . _____	cubs centers
5. The baby bears got up and _____ . _____	laced danced
6. Then, they saw a camel _____ . _____	race mice
7. They tried cotton _____ for the first time. _____	candy ice
8. They hated to go back home to the _____ . _____	car city

Unit 1
Core Skills Phonics, Grade 2

Sounds of g

When **g** is before **e**, **i**, or **y**, it can stand for the **j** sound in **jet**. The letters **dge** stand for the **j** sound, too.

gas **g**em ju**dge**

Name the first picture in each row. Circle the pictures that have the same **g** sound as the first picture.

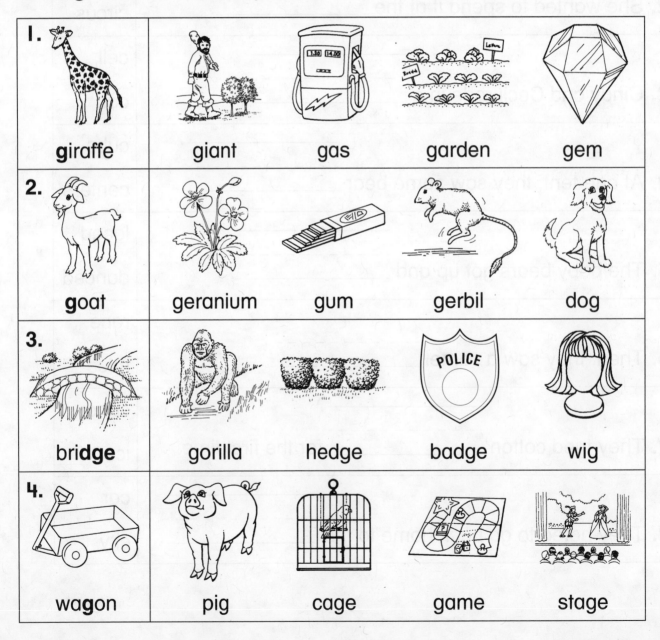

1.				
giraffe	giant	gas	garden	gem
2.				
goat	geranium	gum	gerbil	dog
3.				
bri**dge**	gorilla	hedge	badge	wig
4.				
wa**g**on	pig	cage	game	stage

16

Sounds of g, p. 2

Use a word from the box to answer each clue. Write the word in the puzzle on the lines. Read down the letters in the box to answer the question.

fudge	gerbil	giant	goldfish
hedge	page	pig	stage

1. A big, big man   _ _ _ _ _

2. A farm animal that says "oink"   _ _ _

3. A small pet   _ _ _ _ _ _

4. A part of a book   _ _ _ _

5. A sweet candy   _ _ _ _ _

6. A pet that swims   _ _ _ _ _ _ _ _

7. A fence made of plants   _ _ _ _ _

8. A place for a play   _ _ _ _ _

What are the tallest animals in the world?

_ _ _ _ _ _ _ _

Sounds of g in Context

Read each sentence. Circle the word that completes the sentence.
Write it on the line.

1. A _____ lives in the city.	game giant
2. He has a big, big _____.	gate huge
3. He works out in a big, big _____.	gym gum
4. His pet is a _____.	giraffe hedge
5. One day, the _____ came to visit.	general cage
6. She needed some _____.	page gas
7. The giant _____ her some.	badge gave
8. "You are a _____!" she said.	gem go

Sounds of s

In **sun**, **s** stands for the **s** sound.
In **rose**, **s** stands for the **z** sound.
In **sugar**, **s** stands for the **sh** sound.

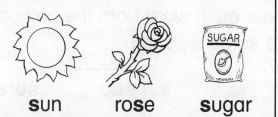

sun ro**s**e **s**ugar

Write **s**, **z**, or **sh** on the line to tell the sound that **s** stands for in each picture name.

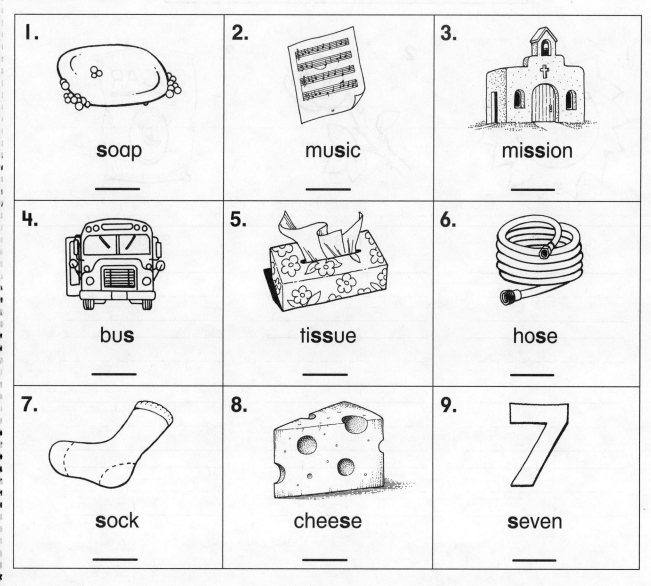

1.	2.	3.
soap	mu**s**ic	mi**ss**ion
____	____	____
4.	5.	6.
bu**s**	ti**ss**ue	ho**s**e
____	____	____
7.	8.	9.
sock	chee**s**e	**s**even
____	____	____

Name _____ Date _____

Sounds of s̲, p. 2

Write each word from the box under the picture with the name that has the same **s** sound.

see	surely	us	wise
tissue	please	side	his
nose	seven	issue	sure

1.

sun

_ _ _ _ _ _ _ _ _ _ _

_ _ _ _ _ _ _ _ _ _ _

_ _ _ _ _ _ _ _ _ _ _

_ _ _ _ _ _ _ _ _ _ _

2.

rose

_ _ _ _ _ _ _ _ _ _ _

_ _ _ _ _ _ _ _ _ _ _

_ _ _ _ _ _ _ _ _ _ _

_ _ _ _ _ _ _ _ _ _ _

3.

sugar

_ _ _ _ _ _ _ _ _ _ _

_ _ _ _ _ _ _ _ _ _ _

_ _ _ _ _ _ _ _ _ _ _

_ _ _ _ _ _ _ _ _ _ _

Sounds of s in Context

Read each sentence. Circle the word that completes the sentence.
Write it on the line.

1. Sue _____ has a bad cold.	sun surely
2. Her _____ is all red.	song nose
3. It is as red as a _____.	mission rose
4. Sue needs more _____.	tissues hoses
5. _____ get her a new box.	Please This
6. Poor Sue! Is her throat _____, too?	sit sore
7. Sue can _____ a long rest.	use rise
8. I'm _____ that will cure her cold.	sugar sure

Name _____ Date _____

Review Sounds of <u>c</u>, <u>g</u>, and <u>s</u>

Read each sentence. Write the sentence that tells about the picture.

1. Carmen sees the giraffe.
   Carmen sees the geese.

_____

- -

2. Sam has a rose garden.
   Sam soaps his car.

_____

_____

3. Gina goes to the sea.
   Gina gets a pet gerbil.

_____

- -

4. The goat hops over a fence.
   The goat eats the grass.

_____

- -

Review Sounds of <u>c</u>, <u>g</u>, and <u>s</u>, p. 2

Circle the word that names the picture. Write it on the line.

1. Is it a **stage**, **page**, or **huge**?		_____
2. Is it a **jar**, **car**, or **star**?		_____
3. Is it a **gym**, **jam**, or **game**?	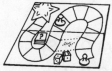	_____
4. Is it a **judge**, **fudge**, or an **edge**?		_____
5. Is it a **bus**, **bug**, or **budge**?		_____
6. Is it a **rose**, **hose**, or **nose**?		_____
7. Is it the **sun**, **sugar**, or **sure**?		_____
8. Is it **nice**, **dice**, or **mice**?		_____

23

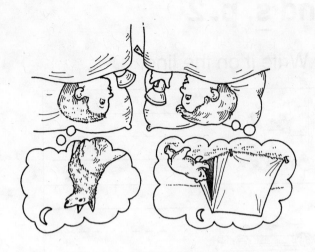

Is it a bear cub?
Is it a wild wolf?

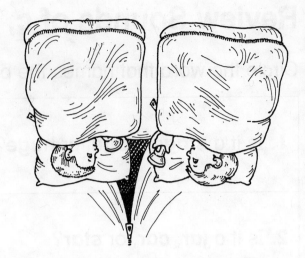

George and Sam camp out
in the backyard. They hear
a sound.

The boys peek out. It is just a

_____

_____ .

Camping Out

Finish the story. Tell what the
boys see. Draw a picture.

_____
made this book!

Name _____ Date _____

Quiz Yourself!

Name each picture. Circle the letter that stands for the **missing** sound.
Write the answer on the line.

1. g b k ro __ ot	**2.** f t l lea __	**3.** b p d __ og
4. p t b mo __	**5.** l w r __ ake	**6.** n m r ha __
7. g c s __ oat	**8.** n r m fa __	**9.** h t l sa __ ad
10. l n b __ ug	**11.** f t l wa __ er	**12.** w v r __ ig

Unit 1
Core Skills Phonics, Grade 2

Name _____ Date _____

Quiz Yourself!, p. 2

Name each picture. Circle the letter that completes the word. Write the answer on the line.

1. b d g we___	**2.** b g r ja___	**3.** m d s me___al
4. l s d ___ock	**5.** m s c i___e	**6.** b g m ___oat
7. h g d ___em	**8.** k b t for___	**9.** b f m ___an
10. g j s bad___e	**11.** z s m ho___e	**12.** c s f pen___il

Unit 1
Core Skills Phonics, Grade 2

Name _____ Date _____

Unit I Assessment

Name each picture. Circle the letter that completes the word. Write the answer on the line.

1. d s c z i__e	**2.** f m d b ca__in	**3.** l s d t ru__er
4. t d c s __ea	**5.** r t n g fi__	**6.** g t n r ba__
7. b t c h __orn	**8.** g b d t __as	**9.** b f r s __un
10. h g d j __iraffe	**11.** z d s b ro__e	**12.** w v m n __atch

27

© Houghton Mifflin Harcourt Publishing Company

Unit 1
Core Skills Phonics, Grade 2

Unit 1 Assessment, p. 2

Fill in the circle next to the word that completes each sentence.

1. A zookeeper came to our school with a ____.
   - ○ came
   - ○ cage
   - ○ care
   - ○ cake

2. She works at the zoo in the ____.
   - ○ city
   - ○ site
   - ○ sit
   - ○ cat

3. She brought a ____!
   - ○ goal
   - ○ goat
   - ○ glow
   - ○ gone

4. We played with it in the school ____.
   - ○ gym
   - ○ gas
   - ○ get
   - ○ germ

5. It was ____ to pet it.
   - ○ share
   - ○ safe
   - ○ same
   - ○ sad

6. The zookeeper invited us to ____ the zoo.
   - ○ camel
   - ○ visit
   - ○ lemon
   - ○ cabin

7. I had fun at the ____.
   - ○ too
   - ○ zoo
   - ○ zip
   - ○ shoe

8. We rode on a ____.
   - ○ bug
   - ○ bus
   - ○ bun
   - ○ bud

9. The ____ was hot.
   - ○ fun
   - ○ run
   - ○ sun
   - ○ bun

10. We saw a big ____.
    - ○ tiger
    - ○ cut
    - ○ razor
    - ○ lemon

11. We saw a ____, too.
    - ○ seat
    - ○ meal
    - ○ seal
    - ○ sea

12. It splashed ____ on us!
    - ○ wagon
    - ○ water
    - ○ wag
    - ○ wheel

Hearing Short Vowel <u>a</u>

If a word has only one vowel,
the vowel sound is usually short.
Short a is the vowel sound you
hear in **ant** and **cap**.

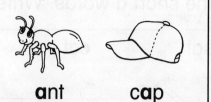

ant   c**a**p

Name each picture. If you hear the short **a** sound, write **a** on the line.

I. _____	2. _____	3. _____	4. _____
5. _____	6. _____	7. _____	8. _____
9. _____	10. _____	II. _____	I2. _____

Name _____ Date _____

Writing Short Vowel a Words

Read the short **a** words. Write the word that names each picture.

1.	sat	cat	mat	bat	hat

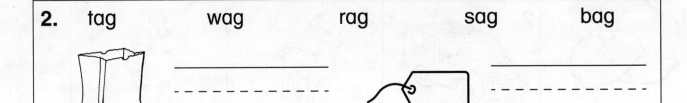

2.	tag	wag	rag	sag	bag

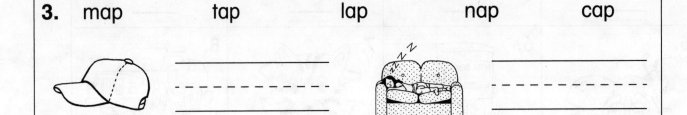

3.	map	tap	lap	nap	cap

4.	yam	dam	ram	ham	jam

5.	fan	ran	can	man	pan

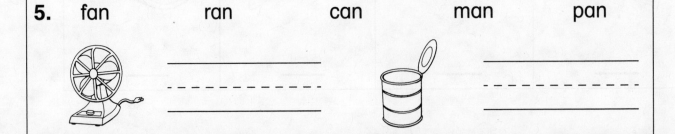

Name _____ Date _____

Hearing Short Vowel i

If a word has only one vowel,
the vowel sound is usually short.
Short i is the vowel sound you
hear in **ink** and **pig**.

 ink   pig

Name each picture. If you hear the short **i** sound, write **i** on the line.

1.	2.	3.	4.
___	___	___	___
5.	6.	7.	8.
___	___	___	___
9.	10.	11.	12.
___	___	___	___

31

© Houghton Mifflin Harcourt Publishing Company

Unit 2
Core Skills Phonics, Grade 2

Name _____   Date _____

Writing Short Vowel i Words

Read the short **i** words. Write the word that names each picture.

1.	will	ill	fill	hill	mill

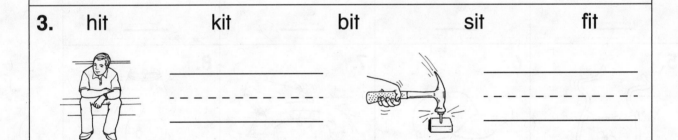

2.	kid	did	rid	lid	hid

3.	hit	kit	bit	sit	fit

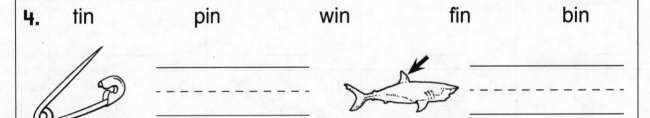

4.	tin	pin	win	fin	bin

5.	dig	pig	wig	fig	big

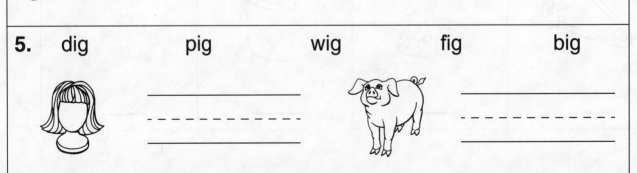

32

Hearing Short Vowel <u>o</u>

> If a word has only one vowel,
> the vowel sound is usually short.
> **Short o** is the vowel sound you
> hear in **ox** and **dog**.
>
>
>
> **ox**   **dog**

Name each picture. If you hear the short **o** sound, write **o** on the line.

1. ___	2. ___	3. ___	4. ___
5. ___	6. ___	7. ___	8. ___
9. ___	10. ___	11. ___	12. ___

33

Writing Short Vowel o Words

Read the short **o** words. Write the word that names each picture.

1. lock	mock	rock	sock	dock

_____

_____

2. cob	sob	job	rob	mob

_____

_____

3. box	fox	lox	ox	pox

_____

_____

4. cot	not	hot	dot	tot

_____

_____

5. hop	pop	mop	cop	top

_____

_____

34

Hearing Short Vowel u

> If a word has only one vowel,
> the vowel sound is usually short.
> **Short u** is the vowel sound you
> hear in **up** and **bug**.

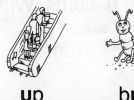

up   b**u**g

Name each picture. If you hear the short **u** sound, write **u** on the line.

1.	2.	3.	4.
___	___	___	___

5.	6.	7.	8.
___	___	___	___

9.	10.	11.	12.
___	___	___	___

Name _____ Date _____

Writing Short Vowel u Words

Read the short **u** words. Write the word that names each picture.

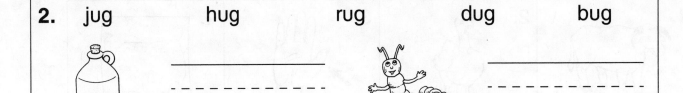

1.	fun	run	gun	sun	bun

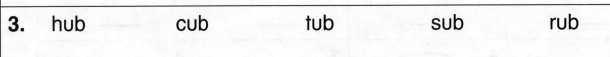

2.	jug	hug	rug	dug	bug

3.	hub	cub	tub	sub	rub

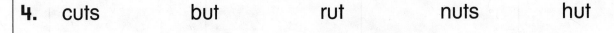

4.	cuts	but	rut	nuts	hut

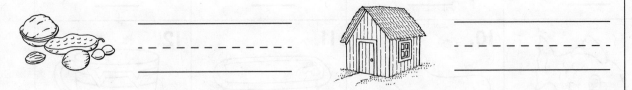

5.	luck	duck	buck	tuck	puck

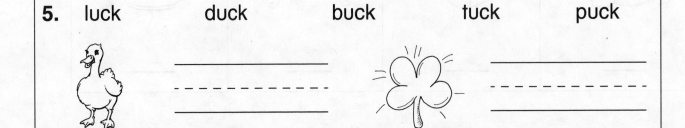

36

Hearing Short Vowel e

If a word has only one vowel,
the vowel sound is usually short.
Short e is the vowel sound you
hear in **egg** and **nest**.

 **e**gg

  n**e**st

Name each picture. If you hear the short **e** sound, write **e** on the line.

1.	2.	3.	4.
___	___	___	___
5.	6.	7.	8.
___	___	___	___
9.	10.	11.	12.
___	___	___	___

37

Writing Short Vowel e Words

Read the short **e** words. Write the word that names each picture.

1. dent   went   rent   tent   cent

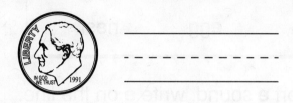 _ _ _ _ _ _ _ _ _ _ _   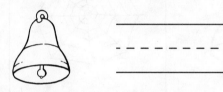 _ _ _ _ _ _ _ _ _ _ _

2. bell   well   sell   fell   yell

 _ _ _ _ _ _ _ _ _ _ _   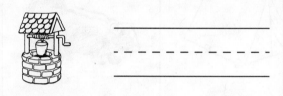 _ _ _ _ _ _ _ _ _ _ _

3. test   best   vest   west   nest

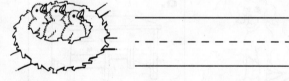 _ _ _ _ _ _ _ _ _ _ _   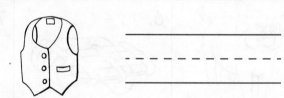 _ _ _ _ _ _ _ _ _ _ _

4. keg   leg   peg   egg   beg

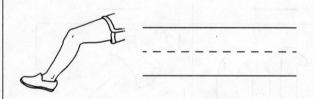 _ _ _ _ _ _ _ _ _ _ _   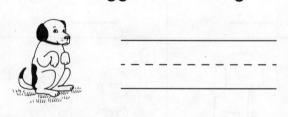 _ _ _ _ _ _ _ _ _ _ _

5. yet   net   jet   pet   let

 _ _ _ _ _ _ _ _ _ _ _    _ _ _ _ _ _ _ _ _ _ _

38

Review Short Vowels

Name the vowel and the first picture in each row. Color the pictures that have the same short vowel sound as the first picture.

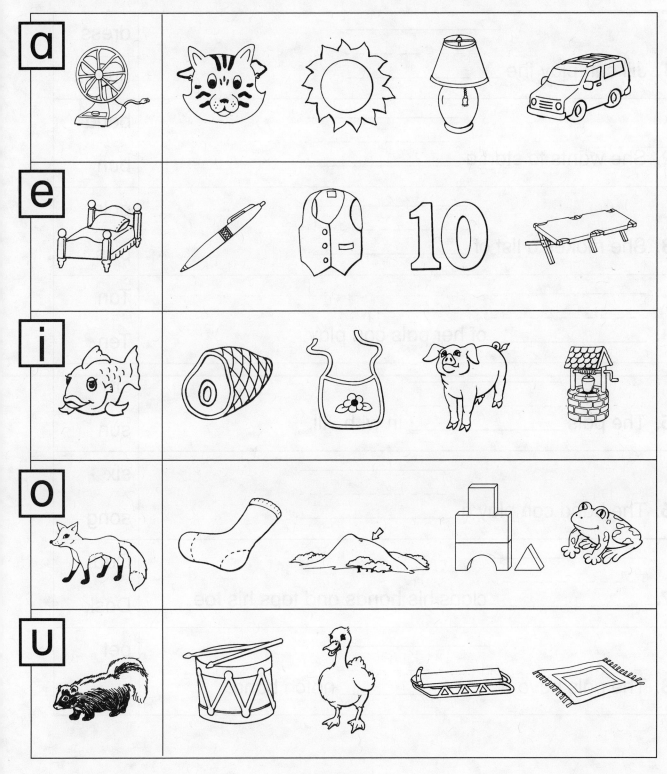

Review Short Vowels in Context

Read each sentence. Circle the word that completes the sentence. Write it on the line.

1. Jill can play the _____.	dress drums
2. She wants to start a _____.	band bun
3. She makes a list of _____.	pals pills
4. _____ of her pals can play.	Tan Ten
5. The pals _____ in with Jill.	sit sun
6. The band can play a _____.	six song
7. _____ claps his hands and taps his toe.	Dad Desk
8. The pals have a _____ notch band.	pet top

40

Name _____ Date _____

Review Short Vowels: Mystery Vowel

Write the same vowel in each word to complete the sentence.

1. The d___cks had f___n in the wet m___d.

2. The c___t s___t on Tom's l___p.

3. A girl wants to g___t a p___t h___n.

4. The d___g h___ps ___n the l___g.

5. W___ll J___m's b___g f___sh w___n?

Unit 2
Core Skills Phonics, Grade 2

Reading Comprehension: Short Vowels

Circle the sentence that tells about the picture.

1. Sandy's hat fell.

A ball hits Sandy.

Sandy wants to get a hat.

2. Tess wants to sell a hat.

Tess sells pots and pans.

Tess sells hens and ducks.

3. Sandy sits on a cot.

Sandy puts on a hat.

Tess gets a big hat box.

4. The hat is big.

The hat has mud on it.

The hat is small.

5. It's fun to get a hat.

It's fun to get a hit.

It's fun to get a pup.

Hearing Long Vowel <u>a</u>

- **Ax** has the **short a** sound.

- **Rake** has the **long a** sound.

Color the picture if its name has the long **a** sound.

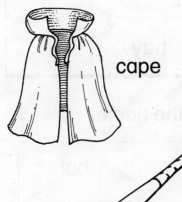
cape

cap

game

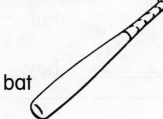
bat

jay

cake

tape

pail

cane
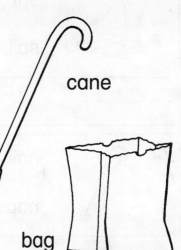

vase
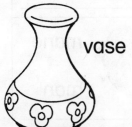

can

bag

Unit 2
Core Skills Phonics, Grade 2

Name _____ Date _____

Writing Long Vowel <u>a</u> Words

A vowel usually has the long sound when a consonant and **e** come after it. The **e** is silent.

When two vowels are together, the first vowel usually has the long sound. The second vowel is silent.

You can hear the **long a** sound in **rake**, **rain**, and **hay**.

ra**ke**   **r**a**in**   **h**a**y**

Name each picture. Circle the picture name. Write the name.

1.  gate gap	2.  mail mall	3.  hat hay
4. sat sail	5. tape tap	6.  bat bait
7. nail nap	8. ran rain	9. mane man

© Houghton Mifflin Harcourt Publishing Company

Unit 2
Core Skills Phonics, Grade 2

Name _____ Date _____

Hearing Long Vowel <u>i</u>

> • **Pig** has the **short i** sound   • **Kite** has the **long i** sound.

Color the picture if its name has the long **i** sound.

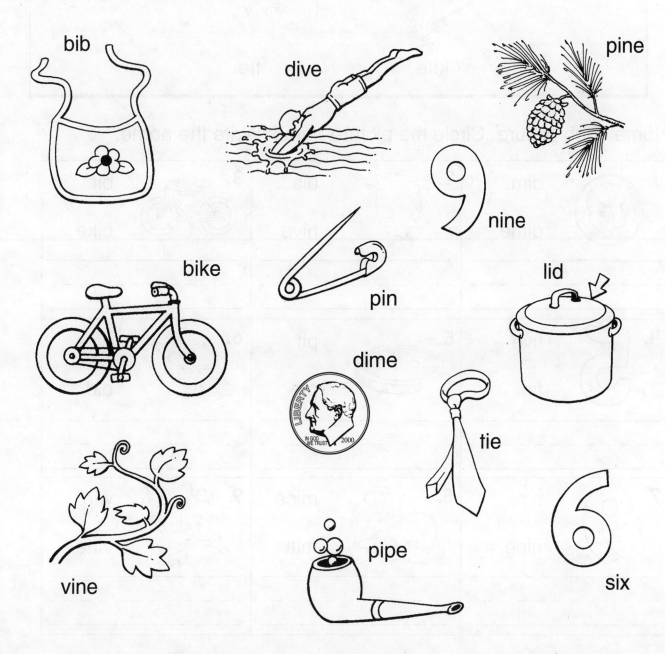

bib

dive

pine

nine

bike

pin

lid

dime

tie

vine

pipe

six

45

© Houghton Mifflin Harcourt Publishing Company

Unit 2
Core Skills Phonics, Grade 2

Writing Long Vowel i Words

A vowel usually has the long sound when a consonant and **e** come after it. The **e** is silent.

When two vowels are together, the first vowel usually has the long sound. The second vowel is silent.

You can hear the **long i** sound in **kite** and **tie**.

kite   **tie**

Name each picture. Circle the picture name. Write the name.

1. dim / dime	**2.** his / hive	**3.** bit / bike
4. five / fin	**5.** pit / pie	**6.** dive / did
7. nip / nine	**8.** mice / mitt	**9.** win / vine

46

Hearing Long Vowel <u>o</u>

• **Fox** has the **short o** sound.   • **Goat** has the **long o** sound.

Color the picture if its name has the long **o** sound.

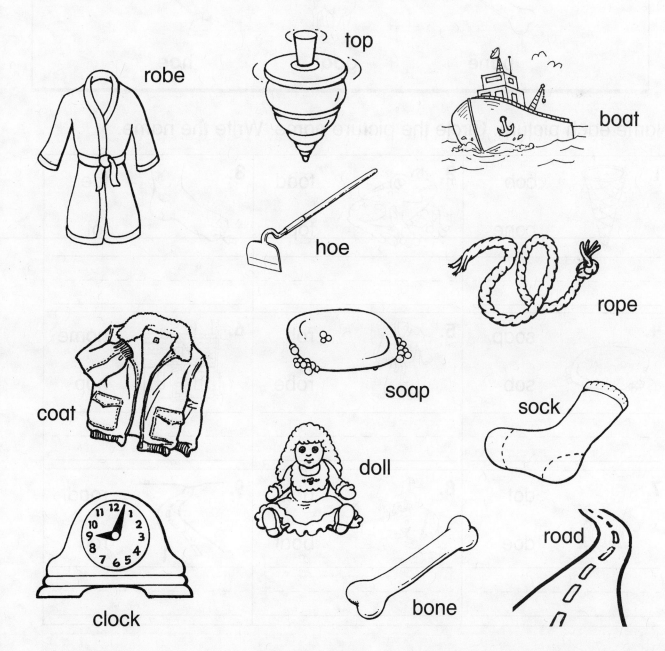

robe

top

boat

hoe

rope

coat

soap

sock

doll

clock

bone

road

Name _____ Date _____

Writing Long Vowel o Words

A vowel usually has the long sound when a consonant and **e** come after it. The **e** is silent.

When two vowels are together, the first vowel usually has the long sound. The second vowel is silent.

You can hear the **long o** sound in **bone**, **goat**, and **hoe**.

bo**ne**   **g**o**a**t   **h**o**e**

Name each picture. Circle the picture name. Write the name.

1.	cob cone	2.	toad top	3.	toe tot
4.	soap sob	5.	rob robe	6.	home hop
7.	dot doe	8.	box boat	9.	road rod

Unit 2
Core Skills Phonics, Grade 2

Hearing Long Vowel _u_

> • **Cub** has the **short u** sound.   • **Cube** has the **long u** sound.

Color the picture if its name has the long **u** sound.

tune

cup

mule

bug

June

ruler

duck

flute

tube

prune

sun

fuse

© Houghton Mifflin Harcourt Publishing Company

Unit 2
Core Skills Phonics, Grade 2

Writing Long Vowel u Words

A vowel usually has the long sound when a consonant and **e** come after it. The **e** is silent. You can hear the **long u** sound in **cube**.

cube

Name each picture. Circle the picture name. Write the name.

1. plume / plum	**2.** flute / full	**3.** fumes / fun
4. Jud / June	**5.** mutt / mule	**6.** put / prune
7. dune / dust	**8.** fuss / fuse	**9.** tube / tub

Hearing Long Vowel e

- **Bed** has the **short e** sound.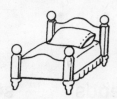
- **Beads** has the **long e** sound.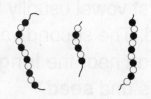

Color the picture if its name has the long **e** sound.

team

web

jeep

meat

net

queen

bee

seal

bed

feet

leg

beak

51

Writing Long Vowel e Words

When two vowels are together, the first vowel usually has the long sound. The second vowel is silent. You can hear the **long e** sound in **beads** and **seed**.

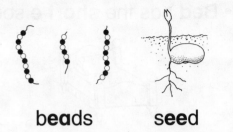

beads   seed

Name each picture. Circle the picture name. Write the name.

1. jet / jeep	**2.** tea / test	**3.** bed / bee
4. seal / seed	**5.** quest / queen	**6.** meat / met
7. weed / wed	**8.** peas / pest	**9.** ten / team

52

Writing Words with y as a Vowel

At the end of a short word, like **fly**, **y** stands for the **long i** sound.
At the end of a longer word, like **twenty**, **y** stands for the **long e** sound.

fly   twenty

Say and write each picture name. Write **y** to finish each word. Color the picture red if **y** has the vowel sound in **fly**. Color the picture green if **y** has the vowel sound in **twenty**.

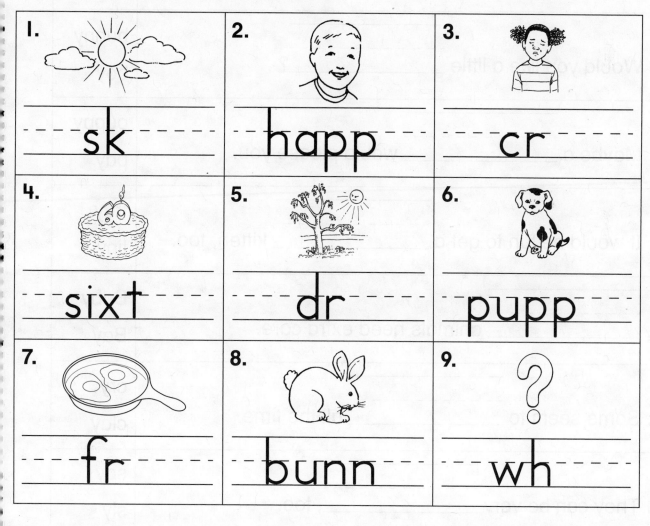

1. sk____

2. happ____

3. cr____

4. sixt____

5. dr____

6. pupp____

7. fr____

8. bunn____

9. wh____

y as a Vowel in Context

Read each sentence. Circle the word that completes the sentence.
Write it on the line.

1. What kind of pet would make you _____?	hay happy
2. My pal Penny has _____ little fish.	twenty try
3. Would you like a little _____?	bunny boy
4. Maybe a _____ would please you.	puppy pay
5. It would be fun to get a _____ kitten, too.	tray tiny
6. _____ animals need extra care.	Baby Bay
7. Some seem to _____ all the time.	cry clay
8. They can be very _____, too.	say sly

Name _____ Date _____

Review Long Vowels and <u>y</u>

Name each picture. Circle the picture name. Write the name.

1. met / meat	**2.**  tie / toe	**3.** rain / ran
4. 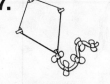 cane / can	**5.** 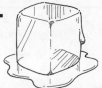 free / fry	**6.** got / goat
7. kite / kit	**8.** cube / cub	**9.** wed / weed
10. robe / rob	**11.** plane / plan	**12.**  by / bay

Unit 2
Core Skills Phonics, Grade 2

Name _____ Date _____

Review Long Vowels and y in Context

Read each sentence. Write the sentence that tells about the picture.

1. Bees like nice tiny buds.
Bees are at home in a hive.

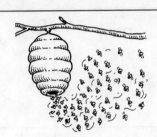

_____

- -

_____

2. Jay can play the flute.
Jay can use the hose.

_____

- -

_____

3. The goat eats the rose.
The baby mule is cute.

_____

- -

_____

4. Dad tries to bake a lime pie.
Dad cooks meat on the grill.

_____

- -

_____

Review Long Vowels

Name the vowel and the first picture in each row. Color the pictures that have the same long vowel sound as the first picture.

Reading Comprehension: Long Vowels

Read the story. Choose the best title and circle it. Write it on this line.

_____

- -

_____

"I made the team!" yelled Jean.

"Way to go!" said Lee. "It will be fun to see you play ball."

Lee came to see Jean's game. As Lee sat in his seat, the ump yelled, "Play ball!"

"Hit a home run!" screamed Lee. But Jean did not hit the ball.

"Strike one!" called the ump.

Jean looked at the sky. She hoped for rain. "Use your brain!" screamed Lee.

Jean tried her best. She waited for a good ball. When it came, Jean swung. She hit a home run.

"Safe at home," called the ump.

"Hooray for Jean!" the team yelled. "They cannot beat us with Jean on the team."

A Long Fly Ball

Jean's Team Cannot Win

Jean Hits a Home Run

Hearing r-Controlled Vowel ar

When **r** follows a vowel, it changes the vowel sound. You can hear the **ar** sound in **car**. The vowel is neither long nor short.

car

Say each picture name. Color the pictures that have the **ar** sound.

Hearing and Writing r-Controlled Vowel ar

Name each picture. Write **ar** if you hear the same vowel sound as in **car**.

1.	2.	3.	4.
st__	sh__k	m__l	h__p

5.	6.	7.	8.
b__k	j__	y__n	b__d

9.	10.	11.	12.
f__k	b__n	b__n	__m

Name _____ Date _____

Hearing r-Controlled Vowel or

When **r** follows a vowel, it changes the vowel sound. You can hear the **or** sound in **corn**. The vowel is neither long nor short.

c**or**n

Say each picture name. Color the pictures that have the **or** sound.

61

© Houghton Mifflin Harcourt Publishing Company

Core Skills Phonics, Grade 2

Hearing and Writing r-Controlled Vowel or

Name each picture. Write **or** if you hear the same vowel sound as in **corn**.

1.  t__ch	2.  t__tle	3.  h__se	4.  st__k
5.  d__t	6.  h__n	7.  c__k	8.  p__ch
9.  n__se	10.  f__ty	11. 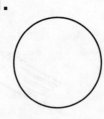 c__cle	12.  f__k

Hearing and Writing r-Controlled Vowels ur, ir, and er

The letter pairs **ur**, **ir**, and **er** all have the same sound. You can hear this sound in **church**, **bird**, and **herd**. The vowel is neither short nor long.

ch**ur**ch   b**ir**d   h**er**d

Write a word from the box to name each picture.

nurse	purse	surf	girl	shirt	skirt	stir	twirl	fern

1.	2.	3.
_____ - - - - - - _____	_____ - - - - - - _____	_____ - - - - - - _____
4.	5.	6.
_____ - - - - - - _____	_____ - - - - - - _____	_____ - - - - - - _____
7.	8.	9.
_____ - - - - - - _____	_____ - - - - - - _____	_____ - - - - - - _____

Hearing and Writing r-Controlled Vowels ur, ir, and er, p. 2

Use a word from the box to answer each riddle. Write the word on the line.

bird	burns	circle	fern	fur	herd	letter	purse

1. Many animals have this.

_____

2. This is a kind of plant.

_____

3. You can write and mail this.

_____

4. A woman can carry money in this.

_____

5. A fire does this.

_____

6. This is a group of cows.

_____

7. This shape is round.

_____

8. This animal can fly.

_____

Name _____ Date _____

Review r-Controlled Vowels

Name each picture. Circle the picture name. Write the name.

1.  surf skirt _____ _ _ _ _ _	**2.**  fork first _____ _ _ _ _ _	**3.**  short shirt _____ _ _ _ _ _
4. germ girl _____ _ _ _ _ _	**5.**  herd harm _____ _ _ _ _ _	**6.**  burn barn _____ _ _ _ _ _
7. car cord _____ _ _ _ _ _	**8.** form fern _____ _ _ _ _ _	**9.**  born bird _____ _ _ _ _ _
10.  horn hurt _____ _ _ _ _ _	**11.** scarf star _____ _ _ _ _ _	**12.**  church shark _____ _ _ _ _ _

Review: Classifying r-Controlled Vowels

Circle the words that belong.

1. Which are places?

barn	burn	church	park	pork
fort	fork	yard	yarn	born

2. Which are animals?

stork	start	short	shark	horse
horn	bird	bark	sharp	shirt

3. Which can you hear?

horn	snarl	harm	organ	harp
chirp	part	purr	smart	snort

4. Which are on a farm?

born	barn	horse	hard	corn
word	dirt	park	dark	herd

5. Which can you wear?

sport	spur	shorts	storm	scarf
star	stern	shirt	fork	skirt

Unit 2
Core Skills Phonics, Grade 2

Review r-Controlled Vowels: Letter Logic

Use the clues to find the mystery picture. Write the name of the picture on the line. Color the picture.

Hint: Cross out the pictures as you solve the clues.

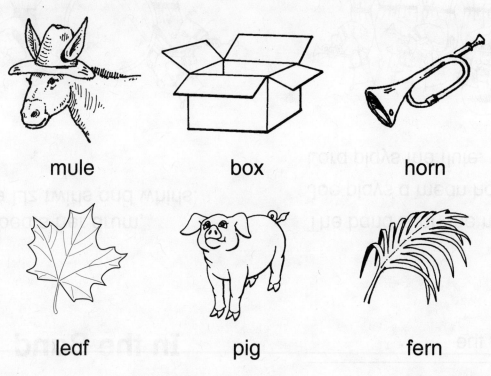

mule	box	horn
leaf	pig	fern

It does **not** have a short vowel sound.

It does **not** end with **f**.

It does **not** start with **f**.

It is **not** the name of an animal.

It **does** have a vowel with **r**.

It is _____.

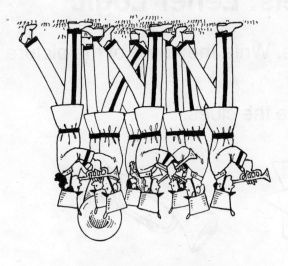

Lora plays the flute.
Joe plays a mean horn.
The band is on the march.

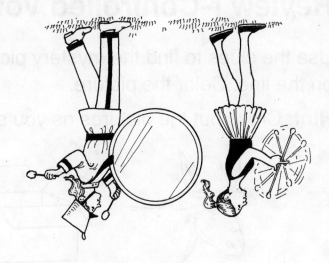

Jen beats her drum,
while Liz twirls and whirls.

And I play the

_____

– –

_____ .

In the Band

_____
made this book!

Finish the story. Tell what you want to play. Draw its picture.

Name _____ Date _____

Quiz Yourself!

Name each picture. Circle the letter or letters that complete the word.
Write the answer on the line.

1.	i o u	2.	y ee u	3.	y_e u_e a_y
b__x		sk__		m__l__	

4.	ar or ir	5.	e a i	6.	oo ai oa
b___n		h__t		g___t	

7.	er or ir	8.	i_e y_e o_e	9.	a_e u_e o_e
f___k		r__p__		c__k__	

10.	o u e	11.	ee ei oa	12.	or ur ir
d__ck		p___l		b___d	

Unit 2
Core Skills Phonics, Grade 2

Name _____ Date _____

Quiz Yourself!, p. 2

Read each sentence. Fill in the circle next to the word that completes the sentence.

1. Rob is going to _____ in a plane.
   - ○ five
   - ○ fly
   - ○ face

2. It will be a long _____.
   - ○ try
   - ○ toe
   - ○ trip

3. Grandma will _____ him after he lands.
   - ○ meet
   - ○ mat
   - ○ must

4. Rob has to _____.
   - ○ pail
   - ○ pack
   - ○ pie

5. What will he _____?
   - ○ tie
   - ○ time
   - ○ take

6. He will miss his _____.
   - ○ puppy
   - ○ web
   - ○ lock

7. The trip is _____ days away.
   - ○ fine
   - ○ six
   - ○ sock

8. He cannot wait to go up in the _____.
   - ○ hat
   - ○ sit
   - ○ sky

9. In the dark, he may see _____.
   - ○ stars
   - ○ stores
   - ○ parks

10. Flying will make him feel like a _____.
    - ○ board
    - ○ bird
    - ○ barn

11. He will help Grandma _____ apples.
    - ○ pile
    - ○ pale
    - ○ peel

12. They will make an apple _____.
    - ○ pay
    - ○ pie
    - ○ pan

70

Name _____ Date _____

Unit 2 Assessment

Name each picture. Circle the letter or letters that complete the word.
Write the answer on the line.

1.	a i o u	f__n
2.	u o i a	d__g
3.	i e a o	w__b

4.	ar or er ur	f____n
5.	oa ea or oo	h____k
6.	i e o y	fr__

7.	a o u i	r__g
8.	u e a o	g__s
9.	a_e i_e a_r o_r	k__t__

10.	u a o i	t__b
11.	u_e i_e o_e a_e	r__s__
12.	uy oy ay ar	b____

Unit 2 Assessment, p. 2

Read each sentence. Fill in the circle next to the word that completes the sentence.

1. Not all plants ____ outside.
   - ○ grow
   - ○ grape
   - ○ grass
   - ○ graze

2. You can grow some in your ____, too.
   - ○ hot
   - ○ hose
   - ○ home
   - ○ hope

3. Put the ____ in a clean pot.
   - ○ soap
   - ○ seeds
   - ○ side
   - ○ stars

4. Cover them with ____.
   - ○ darts
   - ○ fort
   - ○ dirt
   - ○ dark

5. Your plants ____ sun and water.
   - ○ need
   - ○ neat
   - ○ nice
   - ○ nine

6. But don't ____ too much water.
   - ○ under
   - ○ use
   - ○ up
   - ○ fume

7. Turn the pots every ____.
   - ○ dog
   - ○ dear
   - ○ day
   - ○ dime

8. Then each ____ will get light.
   - ○ side
   - ○ same
   - ○ sit
   - ○ seat

9. You can also ____ plants to keep in your house.
   - ○ big
   - ○ boy
   - ○ bug
   - ○ buy

10. A ____ is a good indoor plant.
    - ○ farm
    - ○ fern
    - ○ germ
    - ○ fork

11. It has small ____ leaves.
    - ○ green
    - ○ grab
    - ○ fry
    - ○ grow

12. You will have a ____ indoor garden.
    - ○ fin
    - ○ fine
    - ○ five
    - ○ file

Unit 2
Core Skills Phonics, Grade 2

Name _____   Date _____

Hearing and Writing Initial s Blends

A **consonant blend** is two or more consonants that are together.
The sounds blend together. Each sound is heard. You can hear a
two-letter **s** blend at the beginning of **skate**, **slide**, **smile**, **snail**,
and **star**.

skate   **sl**ide   **sm**ile   **sn**ail   **st**ar

Name each picture. Listen to the first part of the word. Write the first
two letters.

1.  _____	2.  _____	3. _____
4. _____	5.  _____	6.  _____
7.  _____	8.  _____	9.  _____

Hearing and Writing Initial <u>s</u> Blends and <u>tw</u>

Remember that a **consonant blend** is two or more consonants that are together in a word. The sounds blend together, but each sound is heard. You can hear an **s** blend at the beginning of **scale**, **spider**, and **swing**. You can hear a **tw** blend at the beginning of **twelve**.

scale   **sp**ider   **sw**ing   **tw**elve

Name each picture. Listen to the first part of the word. Write the first two letters.

1.  _____	**2.** 20 _____	**3.** HOME VISITORS _____
4.  _____	**5.**  _____	**6.**  _____
7.  _____	**8.**  _____	**9.** 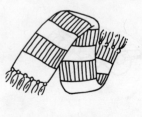 _____

Unit 3
Core Skills Phonics, Grade 2

Name _____ Date _____

Writing Words with Initial s Blends and tw

Name each picture. Circle the picture name. Write the name.

1. 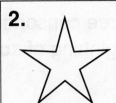 smile slide _____ - - - - - - - - - _____	**2.**  star scar _____ - - - - - - - - - _____	**3.**  twins swans _____ - - - - - - - - - _____
4.  trip twig _____ - - - - - - - - - _____	**5.** stake snake _____ - - - - - - - - - _____	**6.**  skunk drank _____ - - - - - - - - - _____
7. 20 twenty twist _____ - - - - - - - - - _____	**8.** swamp stamp _____ - - - - - - - - - _____	**9.** scale stale _____ - - - - - - - - - _____
10.  spider slide _____ - - - - - - - - - _____	**11.** spoon stone _____ - - - - - - - - - _____	**12.** swing sling _____ - - - - - - - - - _____

Unit 3
Core Skills Phonics, Grade 2

Name _____ Date _____

Hearing and Writing Initial s Blends with Three Letters

Some **consonant blends** have three consonants. You can hear an **s** blend with three letters at the beginning of **screen**, **split**, **spread**, and **street**.

 screen   **spl**it   **spr**ead   **str**eet

Name each picture. Listen to the first part of the word. Write the first three letters.

1.  _____	**2.** _____	**3.**  _____
4.  _____	**5.**  _____	**6.**  _____
7.  _____	**8.**  _____	**9.**  _____

76

Unit 3
Core Skills Phonics, Grade 2

Initial s Blends and tw in Context

Read each sentence. Circle the word that completes the sentence.
Write it on the line.

1. It is fun to look at the _____ . _____	sky scale split
2. In the dark, we see lots of _____ . _____	stars squash springs
3. Those stars really _____ . _____	startle splash sparkle
4. They seem to be on a big movie _____ . _____	skate screen squash
5. If I _____ , the stars seem to spin. _____	twin twirl twelve
6. The moon gives a _____ light, too. _____	strong spunk snip
7. Clouds over the moon look like _____ . _____	smells smoke stops
8. I like to sit on the _____ and look up. _____	spoon string swing

© Houghton Mifflin Harcourt Publishing Company

Unit 3

Core Skills Phonics, Grade 2

Matching Pictures and Sentences

Read each sentence. Write the sentence that tells about the picture.

1. Mom sprays paint on the screen.
   The crew sprays stripes on the street.

_____

_ _

2. We like to skate in the city square.
   We like to splash in the city pool.

_____

_ _

3. Sharon smells a skunk.
   The skunk smells a rose.

_____

_ _

4. The team cannot score in the snow.
   The snowman is wearing Dad's scarf.

_____

_ _

Hearing and Writing Initial r̲ Blends

Remember that a **consonant blend** is two or more consonants that are together. You can hear an **r** blend at the beginning of **bridge**, **crayon**, **dragon**, and **frog**.

bridge

crayon

dragon

frog

Name each picture. Listen to the first part of the word. Write the first two letters.

1. _____	2.  _____	3.  _____
4. 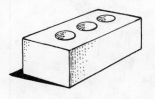 _____	5.  _____	6.  _____
7.  _____	8.  _____	9. 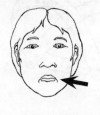 _____

Name _____   Date _____

Hearing and Writing Initial r Blends, p. 2

Remember that a **consonant blend** is two or more consonants
that are together. You can hear an **r** blend at the beginning of
grapes, **price**, and **tractor**.

grapes   **pr**ice   **tr**actor

Name each picture. Listen to the first part of the word. Write the first
two letters.

I.  _____	**2.**  _____	**3.**  _____
4.  _____	**5.** 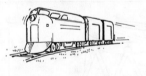 _____	**6.**  _____
7. 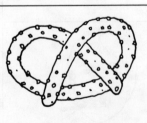 _____	**8.**  _____	**9.**  _____

Name _____ Date _____

Writing Words with Initial r Blends

Name each picture. Circle the picture name. Write the name.

1. raps grapes	**2.** bird brick	**3.** prize rise 
4. crab car	**5.** dorm drum	**6.** train rain
7. frame farm	**8.** girl grill 	**9.** rib crib
10. drill dirt	**11.** fort fruit	**12.** turn truck 

81

Unit 3
Core Skills Phonics, Grade 2

Name _____ Date _____

Initial r Blends in Context

Read each sentence. Circle the word that completes the sentence.
Write it on the line.

_____ - - - - - - - - - - 1. Brad wants to _____.	drip drive
_____ - - - - - - - - - 2. He wants a big _____.	truck track
_____ - - - - - - - - 3. He would load it with _____.	bricks brought
_____ - - - - - - - - - 4. He might load it with _____.	from fruit
_____ - - - - - - - - - 5. Brad would use the _____ to stop.	bring brake
_____ - - - - - - - - - - 6. He would not skid on a wet _____.	bridge broom
_____ - - - - - - - - 7. He would _____ to be the best driver.	try tree
_____ - - - - - - - - - 8. And he would never _____.	crash crown

Hearing and Writing Initial l Blends

Remember that a **consonant blend** is two or more consonants that are together in a word. The sounds blend together, but each sound is heard. You can hear an **l** blend at the beginning of **block**, **clap**, **flag**, **glove**, and **plate**.

 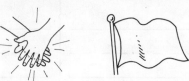

block   **cl**ap   **fl**ag   **gl**ove   **pl**ate

Name each picture. Listen to the first part of the word. Write the first two letters.

1.  _____	**2.**  _____	**3.**  _____
4. 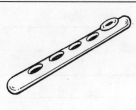 _____	**5.**  _____	**6.**  _____
7.  _____	**8.**  _____	**9.**  _____

Unit 3
Core Skills Phonics, Grade 2

Writing Words with Initial l Blends

Name each picture. Circle the picture name. Write the name.

1. blocks / flocks	**2.** flag / clog	**3.** clock / blink
4. plus / glass	**5.** flip / plop	**6.** flap / clap
7. plane / glow	**8.** blue / flute	**9.** flown / clown
10. glum / plum	**11.** black / brick	**12.** clove / globe

84

© Houghton Mifflin Harcourt Publishing Company

Unit 3
Core Skills Phonics, Grade 2

Writing Words with Initial l Blends, p. 2

Circle the word that names the picture. Write it on the line.

1. Is it a **place**, **plum**, or **palm**?

_____

2. Is it a **fog**, **flip**, or **flag**?

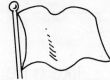

_____

3. Is it a **cloud**, **clown**, or **crown**?

_____

4. Is it a **play**, **pan**, or **plane**?

_____

5. Is it a **globe**, **grab**, or **glow**?

_____

6. Is it **gas**, **glaze**, or a **glass**?

_____

7. Is it **fall**, **float**, or a **fly**?

_____

8. Is it a **clock**, **crow**, or **clue**?

_____

Initial l Blends in Context

Read each sentence. Circle the word that completes the sentence.
Write it on the line.

1. Cleo is a silly _____.	clown / clock
2. She _____ like a hen.	clues / clucks
3. She _____ her arms like wings.	flags / flaps
4. Then she _____ a trick.	plays / plods
5. She pulls an egg out of a clear _____.	glue / glass
6. She cracks the egg on a _____.	play / plate
7. A _____ pops out of the egg.	plant / plead
8. The kids all yell and _____.	clap / class

Review Initial Consonant Blends

Name each picture. Listen to the first part of the word. Write the first two or three letters.

1. _____	2. _____	3. _____
4. _____	5. _____	6. _____
7. _____	8. _____	9. _____
10. _____	11. _____	12. _____
13. _____	14. _____	15. _____

87

Unit 3
Core Skills Phonics, Grade 2

Name _____ Date _____

Review Initial Consonant Blends in Context

Read each sentence. Circle the word that completes the sentence.
Write it on the line.

1. My kite _____ is in the tree.	spray string splash
2. It is wrapped around a _____.	branch brown bright
3. In winter, I like a _____ of warm milk.	glass glaze grape
4. I also play with my _____.	slap sled stripe
5. My dad pulls me with a _____ rope.	strong stroke strum
6. I can see an icicle on every _____.	twelve twenty twig
7. The _____ is thick and white.	snow stove spoon
8. I can _____ the fire in the fireplace.	smile smell small

© Houghton Mifflin Harcourt Publishing Company

Review Initial Consonant Blends: Word Hunt

Find the words from the box in the puzzle. Circle the words. The words go across or down.

bridge	clap	crib	dry	frog
green	play	sleep	stop	try

```
C   L   A   P   L   A   Y

R   S   T   O   P   S   T

I   F   L   Z   X   L   R

B   R   I   D   G   E   Y

R   O   G   R   E   E   N

Z   G   P   Y   Z   P   Y
```

89

Reading Comprehension: Initial Consonant Blends

Read each sentence. Write the sentence that tells about the picture.

1. A skunk sprays if it is scared.
Steve scored the prize goal.

_____

- -

2. Chris plants a tree.
Chris grows big green plants.

_____

- -

3. The baby plays with a stuffed frog.
The baby in the crib is crabby.

_____

- -

4. Cleo brushes and braids her hair.
Cleo cleans the fruit she bought.

_____

- -

Hearing and Writing Final Consonant Blends

A **consonant blend** can also come at the end of a word. You can hear a consonant blend at the end of **nest**, **desk**, **wasp**, **ant**, **jump**, and **hand**.

ne**st**   de**sk**   wa**sp**   a**nt**   ju**mp**   ha**nd**

Name each picture. Listen to the last part of the word. Write the last two letters.

1. 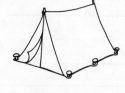 _____	2. _____	3.  _____
4.  _____	5.  _____	6.  _____
7. 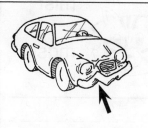 _____	8.  _____	9.  _____

Name _____ Date _____

Writing Words with Final Consonant Blends

Name each picture. Circle the picture name. Write the name.

1. 	2. 	3. 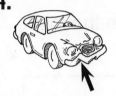
want wrist	plant plump	stamp stand
_____ - - - - - - - - _____	_____ - - - - - - - - _____	_____ - - - - - - - - _____
4. 	5. 	6. 
dent dusk	jump just	tent test
_____ - - - - - - - - _____	_____ - - - - - - - - _____	_____ - - - - - - - - _____
7.	8.	9.
desk dust	band bump	stump stand
_____ - - - - - - - - _____	_____ - - - - - - - - _____	_____ - - - - - - - - _____
10.	11.	12.
mask nest	wasp wand	mist mask
_____ - - - - - - - - _____	_____ - - - - - - - - _____	_____ - - - - - - - - _____

Unit 3

Core Skills Phonics, Grade 2

Final Consonant Blends in Context

Write a word from the box to answer each riddle.

bank	breakfast	damp	fast
stamp	stump	vest	west

1. It is a place to keep money. What is it? _____

2. You put it on a letter. What is it? _____

3. It is a meal. What is it? _____

4. It is the opposite of east. What is it? _____

5. It is a jacket with no sleeves. What is it? _____

6. It is a little bit wet. What is it? _____

7. It is what's left after a tree is cut down. What is it? _____

8. It is the opposite of slow. What is it? _____

Name _____ Date _____

Final Consonant Blends in Context, p. 2

Read each sentence. Write the sentence that tells about the picture.

1. Jan has on the best mask.
Jan has on pants and a vest.

_____

- -

2. Mr. Rusk's tent pole has a big dent.
Mr. Rusk takes the stump off the land.

_____

- -

3. The class cannot stand the band.
The class gives the band a hand.

_____

- -

4. The wasps fly into the nest.
The ants crawl into the plant.

_____

- -

Review Final Consonant Blends

Name each picture. Circle the letters to complete the word. Write the letters on the line.

1.	mp nt sp	2.	nt sp st	3.	nt st sk
ju___		wa___		ne___	

4.	nd st sk	5.	sk st sp	6.	nd st nt
ba___		ve___		ha___	

7.	st sp sk	8.	nt mp nd	9.	nt st mp
de___		te___		la___	

10.	st nd nt	11.	sp mp sk	12.	st sk sp
pla___		cla___		tu___	

Unit 3
Core Skills Phonics, Grade 2

Review Final Consonant Blends in Context

Read each sentence. Circle the word that completes the sentence.
Write it on the line.

1. Randy can _____.	just jump
2. He can run _____.	fast faint
3. Today is the big _____.	test tusk
4. Is Randy the _____?	bunt best
5. Randy goes to _____ at the starting line.	stand stump
6. He runs by all the _____.	rest risk
7. He jumps _____ the best mark.	past plant
8. Randy is the _____.	chant champ

Unit 3

Core Skills Phonics, Grade 2

Review Final Consonant Blends: Word Building

Follow the directions to build each word. Write each new word you make.
Write the last word to answer the question.

1. What **don't** you want on your car? _____

   Start with: **want**

   Change **a** to **e**: _____

   Change **n** to **s**: _____

   Change **w** to **v**: _____

   Change **s** to **n**: _____

   Change **v** to **d**: _____

2. Where do you keep a pet fish? _____

   Start with: **desk**

   Change **e** to **i**: _____

   Change **i** to **u**: _____

   Change **d** to **t**: _____

   Change **u** to **a**: _____

   Change **s** to **n**: _____

3. What is a good thing to keep in your piggy bank? _____

   Start with: **hand**

   Change **h** to **l**: _____

   Change **a** to **e**: _____

   Change **l** to **b**: _____

   Change **d** to **t**: _____

   Change **b** to **c**: _____

made this book!

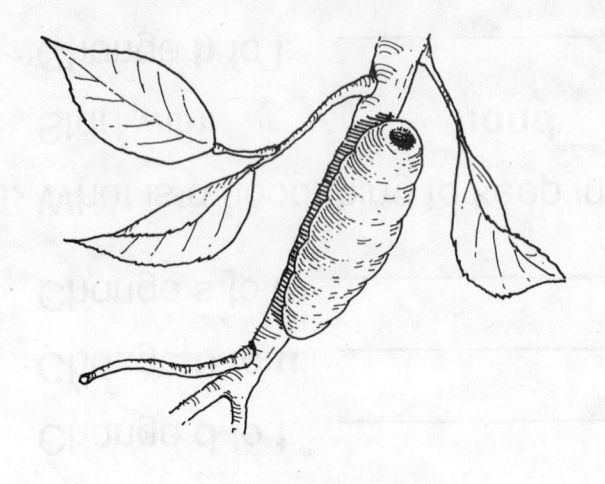

Wasps

What bug do you like? Draw it.

Many wasp families stay in the same nest. Some wasps use a very small stone as a tool.

Most of us can't stand wasps. Wasps can sting. But wasp nests are neat.

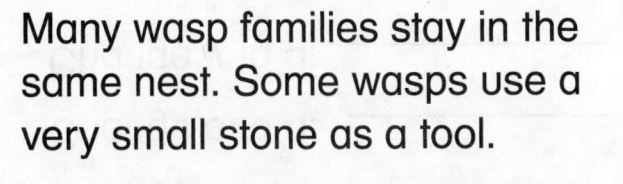

Quiz Yourself!

Name each picture. Circle the blend that completes the word. Write the answer on the line.

1. fr / fl / tr ____uit	**2.** sk / nt / sh te____	**3.** rt / mp / sk ma____
4. sm / sn / tw ____ail	**5.** cl / bl / fl ____ock	**6.** st / sk / tw ____elve
7. cl / dr / st ____ink	**8.** br / fl / cr ____own	**9.** sp / st / sk tu____
10. mp / nt / nk stu____	**11.** mp / sp / nd sa____	**12.** nd / nt / mp sta____

Name _____ Date _____

Quiz Yourself!, p. 2

Read each sentence. Fill in the circle next to the word that completes the sentence.

1. At first, there is just a ____ or two.
   ○ him   ○ hint
   ○ hurt

2. The ____ are not green anymore.
   ○ trees   ○ tents
   ○ trips

3. The ____ are ripe and ready to eat.
   ○ drums   ○ flags
   ○ plums

4. The grass turns ____.
   ○ blown   ○ brown
   ○ block

5. Then, one day the message is ____.
   ○ clear   ○ climb
   ○ grow

6. The wind is ____.
   ○ cost   ○ cone
   ○ cold

7. The ____ is gray.
   ○ stripe   ○ sky
   ○ stem

8. The ____ hunt for nuts to hide.
   ○ strings   ○ stamps
   ○ squirrels

9. The bird ____ is empty.
   ○ nest   ○ name
   ○ nine

10. White frost forms on the ____ outside.
    ○ glaze   ○ grass
    ○ grab

11. We gather ____ for the fireplace.
    ○ twigs   ○ twine
    ○ twelve

12. Mom says, "Better put on a ____. It's fall."
    ○ sweep   ○ sweater
    ○ swan

100

Core Skills Phonics, Grade 2

Name _____ Date _____

Unit 3 Assessment

Name each picture. Circle the blend that completes the word. Write the answer on the line.

1.	bl cr gr fl	__ab
2.	gr br cr fr	__in
3.	sp nt nd lt	wi__
4.	st sl sh sm	__eep
5.	spl squ str scr	__eam
6.	st br cr tr	__ick
7.	gr st tr sn	__uck
8.	sk st fl sl	__ed
9.	sp sw sc br	__an
10.	mp st nt nd	pla__
11.	rt nt st sk	ve__
12.	sk nt mp nd	de__

Unit 3
Core Skills Phonics, Grade 2

Unit 3 Assessment, p. 2

Read each sentence. Fill in the circle next to the word that completes the sentence.

1. Flip was a _____ in a green pond.
   - ○ free
   - ○ flap
   - ○ frog
   - ○ flag

2. He _____ and hopped and ate flies.
   - ○ swam
   - ○ sweet
   - ○ swing
   - ○ swan

3. He could _____ as high as the birds.
   - ○ stump
   - ○ stamp
   - ○ junk
   - ○ jump

4. Flip wanted to _____ like a swan.
   - ○ flag
   - ○ fly
   - ○ crab
   - ○ dry

5. He wanted to feel the _____ on his face.
   - ○ wind
   - ○ wand
   - ○ want
   - ○ wart

6. All _____ could do was hop.
   - ○ Flop
   - ○ Drip
   - ○ Flip
   - ○ Grip

7. Flip did not _____.
   - ○ crimp
   - ○ cry
   - ○ creek
   - ○ crisp

8. He looked at his home in the _____.
   - ○ post
   - ○ port
   - ○ pond
   - ○ pole

9. He used a leaf as a _____.
   - ○ rung
   - ○ raft
   - ○ left
   - ○ ring

10. He floated and tried to _____.
   - ○ rent
   - ○ ramp
   - ○ tent
   - ○ rest

11. He jumped off the leaf and made a _____.
   - ○ splash
   - ○ string
   - ○ strum
   - ○ screen

12. "I'll _____ in the water," he said.
   - ○ glad
   - ○ glide
   - ○ grand
   - ○ grab

Name _____ Date _____

Hearing and Writing Initial Digraphs <u>ch</u> and <u>wh</u>

A **consonant digraph** is two or
more consonants that are together.
They stand for only one sound. You
can hear a consonant digraph at the
beginning of **checkers** and **whale**.

checkers   **wh**ale

Name each picture. Listen to the first part of the word. Write **ch** if
you hear the same first sound as in **checkers**. Write **wh** if you hear
the same first sound as in **whale**.

1. _____	2. _____	3. _____
4. _____	5. _____	6. _____
7. _____	8. _____	9. _____

Unit 4
Core Skills Phonics, Grade 2

Hearing and Writing Initial Digraphs <u>th</u> and <u>sh</u>

A **consonant digraph** is two or more
consonants that are together. They
stand for only one sound. You can hear
a consonant digraph at the beginning
of **them**, **thumb**, and **shell**.

them   **thumb**   **shell**

Name each picture. Listen to the first part of the word. Write **th** if you
hear the same first sound as in **them** or **thumb**. Write **sh** if you hear the
same first sound as in **shell**.

1.	2.	3.
_____	13 _____	_____
4.	5.	6.
_____	_____	_____
7.	8.	9.
_____	30 _____	_____

Unit 4
Core Skills Phonics, Grade 2

Initial Digraphs in Context

Read each sentence. Circle the word that completes the sentence.
Write it on the line.

1. It's fun to go to the _____ _____.	shore chore
2. You can look for _____ or go swimming.	shells wheels
3. If you swim, beware of _____.	sharks chats
4. They are not as big as _____.	cheese whales
5. But their teeth are as sharp as _____.	shoes thorns
6. Most of us do not need to fear _____.	third them
7. Sharks _____ away from people.	shy shin
8. _____ you see a shark fin, leave the sea.	White When

© Houghton Mifflin Harcourt Publishing Company

Unit 4
Core Skills Phonics, Grade 2

Name _____ Date _____

Review Initial Digraphs

Name each picture. Circle the picture name. Write the name.

1. chip / sheep	2.  chick / shack	3.  thorn / when
4. share / chair	5. shell / whale	6. shirt / third
7.  cheese / wheeze	8. chart / shark	9. wheat / cheat
10. thumb / shame	11. them / chin	12. wheel / chill

Review Initial Digraphs in Context

Read each sentence. Circle the word that completes the sentence. Write it on the line.

_____ 1. The _____ went to the circus.	child whip thorn
_____ 2. A clown's red nose began to _____.	chime shine whine
_____ 3. A _____ fell off his car.	sheep whale wheel
_____ 4. The clown pulled out a tiny _____.	phone flop chop
_____ 5. He tripped on his big blue _____.	those shoes shop
_____ 6. The lion tamer snapped his _____.	ship whip wheat
_____ 7. He used a _____ to keep the lion back.	chair share there
_____ 8. The child said, "I _____ I liked the clowns best!"	stink shrink think

Name _____ Date _____

Hearing and Writing Final Digraphs <u>ch</u> and <u>th</u>

Consonant digraphs come at the end of many words. You can hear a consonant digraph at the end of **bench** and **tooth**.

ben**ch**   too**th**

Name each picture. Listen to the last part of the word. Write the last two letters.

1.	2.	3.
_____	_____	_____
4.	5.	6.
_____	_____	_____
7.	8.	9.
_____	_____	_____

108

© Houghton Mifflin Harcourt Publishing Company

Unit 4

Core Skills Phonics, Grade 2

Hearing and Writing Final Digraphs <u>sh</u>, <u>ck</u>, and <u>tch</u>

Consonant digraphs come at the end of many words. Some have three letters. You can hear a consonant digraph at the end of **fish**, **sock**, and **watch**.

fi**sh**   so**ck**   wa**tch**

Name each picture. Listen to the last part of the word. Write the letters that stand for the last sound.

1. _____	2. _____	3. _____
4. _____	5. _____	6. _____
7. _____	8. _____	9. _____

Unit 4
Core Skills Phonics, Grade 2

Hearing and Writing Final Digraphs <u>ng</u> and <u>nk</u>

Consonant digraphs come at the end of many words. You can hear a consonant digraph at the end of **wing** and **sink**.

wi**ng**   si**nk**

Name each picture. Listen to the last part of the word. Write the last two letters.

1.	**2.**	**3.**
_____	_____	_____
4.	**5.**	**6.**
_____	_____	_____
7.	**8.**	**9.**
_____	_____	_____

Unit 4
Core Skills Phonics, Grade 2

Review Final Digraphs

Name each picture. Circle the picture name. Write the name.

1. 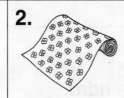 ring / rich	**2.** clash / cloth	**3.** bench / bank
4. tank / tooth	**5.** shock / skunk	**6.** hang / hatch
7. dish / duck	**8.** fang / fish	**9.** wash / watch
10. 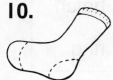 sink / sock	**11.** porch / path	**12.** trunk / track

Unit 4
Core Skills Phonics, Grade 2

Review Final Digraphs in Context

Read each sentence. Circle the word that completes the sentence.
Write it on the line.

_____ I. Life on a _____ can be hard.	tooth ranch
_____ 2. You must _____ the animals all the time.	watch skunk
_____ 3. You must keep cows out of the corn _____.	patch peck
_____ 4. One chore is to _____ the horses.	math brush
_____ 5. There's not much time to rest on the _____.	dish porch
_____ 6. There's no time to _____ in the spring.	fish math
_____ 7. You wish the dinner bell would _____ soon.	hatch ring
_____ 8. Later you crawl off to sleep in your _____.	sink bunk

Unit 4

Core Skills Phonics, Grade 2

Silent Letters <u>wr</u> and <u>kn</u>

Sometimes consonants are **silent**. For example, the **w** in **write** is silent. The word **knight** also has a silent consonant.

write

knight

Name each picture. Listen to the beginning sound. If you hear **r**, as in **write**, write **wr**. If you hear **n**, as in **knight**, write **kn**.

1.	2.	3.
_____	_____	_____

4.	5.	6.
_____	_____	_____

7.	8.	9.
_____	_____	_____

Unit 4
Core Skills Phonics, Grade 2

Writing Words with Silent Letters

Name each picture. Circle the picture name. Write the name.

1. 	note knot	2. 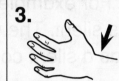	week wreck	3.	whistle wrist
4. 	knee need	5.	knit nice	6. 	rent write
7.	red wrench	8. 	knight nine	9.	neck knock
10.	knife kite	11.	rich wreath	12.	wren went

Unit 4
Core Skills Phonics, Grade 2

Review Final Digraphs and Silent Letters in Context

Fill in the circle next to the word that answers each riddle.

1. Where do strawberries grow?	○ tooth ○ thick ○ patch
2. What will hatch from a hen's egg?	○ thin ○ chick ○ shake
3. What do you hear when a hand hits a door?	○ thing ○ wrist ○ knock
4. How do you get an idea?	○ think ○ shine ○ sing
5. What sound can you make in water?	○ with ○ splash ○ clock
6. What is the name of a tool?	○ wrench ○ ring ○ path
7. What is the opposite of **us**?	○ mush ○ them ○ champ
8. What is the biggest living animal?	○ wren ○ wash ○ whale

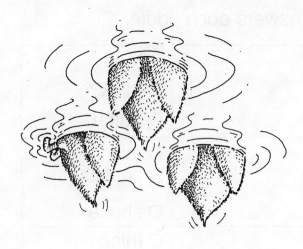

Mom must watch the baby ducks. She must teach them to fish. No! That's all wrong!

They stick in their heads. Now the ducks have the knack.

What did someone teach you?
Write about it. Draw it.

Splish! Splash!

_____

made this book!

Quiz Yourself!

Name each picture. Circle the letters that complete the word. Write the answer on the line.

1.	th ch ck	2.	ck kn wr	3.	sh th tch
ar___		___ench		pa___

4.	wr kn nk	5.	nk ck ng	6.	wr ng kn
___ock		si___		___ite

7.	kn ng nk	8.	nk ck th	9.	th ch sh
___ee		too___		fi___

10.	ch ck ng	11.	ck th ng	12.	wr ng kn
clo___		ki___		___ot

Name _____ Date _____

Quiz Yourself!, p. 2

Read each sentence. Fill in the circle next to the word that completes the sentence.

1. Last summer, I went to a ____.
- ⃝ ranch
- ⃝ rash
- ⃝ rack

2. There was a ____ fence around the ranch.
- ⃝ latch
- ⃝ lace
- ⃝ long

3. The fence was painted ____.
- ⃝ white
- ⃝ whale
- ⃝ chime

4. I saw a ____ of sheep.
- ⃝ flown
- ⃝ flock
- ⃝ flame

5. I saw some ____ in the creek.
- ⃝ fetch
- ⃝ fast
- ⃝ fish

6. I found a wide ____ that led to a creek.
- ⃝ path
- ⃝ patch
- ⃝ pan

7. There were ____ in the bushes.
- ⃝ thorns
- ⃝ storms
- ⃝ bells

8. I fed the ducks some ____.
- ⃝ chores
- ⃝ chins
- ⃝ cheese

9. I followed ____ to the pond.
- ⃝ them
- ⃝ thermos
- ⃝ shoes

10. I was chased by a ____ on my last day.
- ⃝ skunk
- ⃝ skill
- ⃝ trunk

11. I took a ____ after that.
- ⃝ back
- ⃝ bang
- ⃝ bath

12. Next summer, I ____ I will go to a city.
- ⃝ thing
- ⃝ think
- ⃝ thatch

Unit 4
Core Skills Phonics, Grade 2

Unit 4 Assessment

Name each picture. Circle the word that names each picture.

1.	2.	3.
wrench wheat witch what	sheep ship chick cheap	bath bang brick brake

4.	5.	6.
thumb them chat chart	couch chick beach click	skirt shop shirt shine

7.	8.	9.
branch beach bench brand	wheat whale wheel wall	match catch crack watch

10.	11.	12.
whip wipe white wheat	champ chart thorn chore	them with moth moss

Unit 4
Core Skills Phonics, Grade 2

Name _____   Date _____

Unit 4 Assessment, p. 2

Read each sentence. Fill in the circle next to the word that completes the sentence.

1. Patch the Cat thinks she can _____.
   - ○ sink
   - ○ sing
   - ○ sick
   - ○ ship

2. She sings for _____ in the kitchen.
   - ○ chase
   - ○ chimp
   - ○ cheese
   - ○ cheap

3. She sings for fish at _____.
   - ○ lunch
   - ○ lamp
   - ○ luck
   - ○ lump

4. She sings _____ day at dinner.
   - ○ even
   - ○ each
   - ○ bath
   - ○ chick

5. She sings to the little _____ in the window.
   - ○ went
   - ○ wren
   - ○ want
   - ○ wand

6. She sings to the _____ in the bowl.
   - ○ flag
   - ○ fish
   - ○ chimney
   - ○ flip

7. She sings for a _____ of milk.
   - ○ dash
   - ○ ding
   - ○ dish
   - ○ dent

8. She sits on my _____ and sings.
   - ○ knight
   - ○ knee
   - ○ knot
   - ○ nice

9. She sings when I _____ her coat.
   - ○ broom
   - ○ bunk
   - ○ brush
   - ○ bell

10. I _____ she needs to stop singing.
    - ○ think
    - ○ speak
    - ○ shrink
    - ○ thumb

11. Her singing is _____ too loud!
    - ○ much
    - ○ such
    - ○ sock
    - ○ moth

12. I _____ she would just purr.
    - ○ wing
    - ○ wink
    - ○ wish
    - ○ when

120

Answer Key

Page 1
1. *mp* 4. *pl* 7. *tw* 10. *squ*
2. *sk* 5. *spr* 8. *nd* 11. *sw*
3. *tr* 6. *fl* 9. *gr* 12. *sp*

Page 2
1. bench 5. corn
2. wrote 6. boat
3. whale 7. horn
4. chick 8. cute

Page 3
1. *m* 4. *w* 7. *g* 10. *f*
2. *z* 5. *d* 8. *k* 11. *n*
3. *t* 6. *y* 9. *s* 12. *h*

Page 4
1. *j* 5. *v* 9. *t* 13. *d*
2. *f* 6. *l* 10. *s* 14. *m*
3. *p* 7. *r* 11. *w* 15. *b*
4. *h* 8. *c* 12. *b*

Page 5
1. *k* 4. *s* 7. *b* 10. *f*
2. *d* 5. *p* 8. *x* 11. *m*
3. *r* 6. *g* 9. *l* 12. *v*

Page 6
1. *r* 6. *x* 11. *n*
2. *m* 7. *b* 12. *v*
3. *k* 8. *p* 13. *t*
4. *p* or *t* 9. *f* 14. *g*
5. *s* 10. *d* 15. *l* or *t*

Page 7
1. *v* 4. *d* 7. *n*
2. *b* 5. *p* 8. *r*
3. *z* 6. *l* 9. *x*

Page 8
1. *m* 4. *p* 7. *x* 10. *g*
2. *c* 5. *t* 8. *z* 11. *l*
3. *b* 6. *v* 9. *d* 12. *v*

Page 9
1. t_g_r
2. s_l_d
3. c_m_l
4. p_p_r
5. w_g_n
6. b_c_n
7. r_z_r
8. b__v_r
9. f_x_s
10. r_b_n
11. w_m_n
12. d_v_r

Page 10
1. Circle: van, jeep, bike
2. Circle: meat, cake, bun
3. Circle: cub, pup, bud
4. Circle: run, hop, jog
5. Circle: sun, moon, star
6. Circle: hen, goat, pig

Page 11
1. fox 4. van 7. bug
2. cap 5. pig 8. hen
3. log 6. pen

Page 12
The following words should be circled:
1. Rex sees a tub.
2. Rex hides.
3. Pam gets Rex.
4. Rex is wet.
5. Rex gets a prize.

Page 13
The following words should be circled:
1. pencil, fence
2. cap, can
3. lace, ice
4. spruce, face

Page 14
Children should color:
Cecil, lace, groceries, race, city

Page 15
1. cents
2. circus
3. cab
4. cubs
5. danced
6. race
7. candy
8. city

Page 16
1. Circle: giant, gem
2. Circle: gum, dog
3. Circle: hedge, badge
4. Circle: pig, game

Page 17
1. giant
2. pig
3. gerbil
4. page
5. fudge
6. goldfish
7. hedge
8. stage
Answer: giraffes

Page 18
1. giant
2. gate
3. gym
4. giraffe
5. general
6. gas
7. gave
8. gem

Page 19
1. *s* 4. *s* 7. *s*
2. *z* 5. *sh* 8. *z*
3. *sh* 6. *z* 9. *s*

Page 20
1. see, us, side, seven
2. wise, please, his, nose
3. surely, tissue, issue, sure

Page 21
1. surely
2. nose
3. rose
4. tissues
5. Please
6. sore
7. use
8. sure

Page 22
1. Carmen sees the giraffe.
2. Sam soaps his car.
3. Gina goes to the sea.
4. The goat hops over a fence.

Page 23
1. stage
2. car
3. game
4. judge
5. bus
6. nose
7. sugar
8. mice

Page 25
1. *b* 4. *p* 7. *c* 10. *b*
2. *f* 5. *r* 8. *n* 11. *t*
3. *d* 6. *m* 9. *l* 12. *w*

Page 26
1. *b* 4. *s* 7. *g* 10. *g*
2. *r* 5. *c* 8. *k* 11. *s*
3. *d* 6. *g* 9. *f* 12. *c*

Page 27
1. *c* 4. *s* 7. *c* 10. *g*
2. *b* 5. *n* 8. *g* 11. *s*
3. *l* 6. *t* 9. *s* 12. *w*

Page 28
1. cage
2. city
3. goat
4. gym
5. safe
6. visit
7. zoo
8. bus
9. sun
10. tiger
11. seal
12. water

Page 29
Children should write the letter *a* under the following pictures.
1. hat 6. gas 12. ham
2. van 7. mask
5. ant 11. ax

Page 30
1. bat, cat
2. bag, tag
3. cap, nap
4. ram, ham
5. fan, can

Page 31
Children should write the letter *i* under the following pictures.
1. six 5. bib 11. lid
3. wig 7. bridge 12. win
4. fish 9. pin

Page 32
1. hill, mill
2. lid, kid
3. sit, hit
4. pin, fin
5. wig, pig

Page 33
Children should write the letter *o* under the following pictures.
2. frog 6. fox 10. box
3. doll 7. blocks 12. sock
5. clock 8. pot

Page 34
1. rock, sock
2. sob, cob
3. ox, fox
4. cot, dot
5. mop, top

Page 35
Children should write the letter *u* under the following pictures.
2. duck 6. bus 11. tub
3. thumb 7. skunk 12. cup
5. drum 8. gum

Page 36
1. sun, run
2. jug, bug
3. cub, tub
4. nuts, hut
5. duck, luck

Page 37
Children should write the letter *e* under the following pictures.
1. tent 6. sled 10. men
3. bell 8. desk 11. ten
4. web 9. vest

Page 38
1. cent, tent
2. bell, well
3. nest, vest
4. leg, beg
5. pet, net

121

© Houghton Mifflin Harcourt Publishing Company

Page 39

Children should color the following pictures:

a: mask, lamp, van
e: pen, vest, ten
i: bib, pig
o: sock, blocks, frog
u: drum, duck, rug

Page 40

1. drums
2. band
3. pals
4. Ten
5. sit
6. song
7. Dad
8. top

Page 41

1. The ducks had fun in the wet mud.
2. The cat sat on Tom's lap.
3. A girl wants to get a pet hen.
4. The dog hops on the log.
5. Will Jim's big fish win?

Page 42

The following words should be circled:

1. Sandy wants to get a hat.
2. Tess wants to sell a hat.
3. Sandy puts on a hat.
4. The hat is big.
5. It's fun to get a hat.

Page 43

Children should color the following pictures:

cape, game, jay, cake, tape, pail, cane, vase

Page 44

1. gate
2. mail
3. hay
4. sail
5. tape
6. bait
7. nail
8. rain
9. mane

Page 45

Children should color the following pictures:

dive, pine, bike, nine, dime, tie, vine, pipe

Page 46

1. dime
2. hive
3. bike
4. five
5. pie
6. dive
7. nine
8. mice
9. vine

Page 47

Children should color the following pictures:

robe, boat, hoe, rope, coat, soap, bone, road

Page 48

1. cone
2. toad
3. toe
4. soap
5. robe
6. home
7. doe
8. boat
9. road

Page 49

Children should color the following pictures:

tune, June, mule, flute, ruler, tube, prune, fuse

Page 50

1. plume
2. flute
3. fumes
4. June
5. mule
6. prune
7. dune
8. fuse
9. tube

Page 51

Children should color the following pictures:

team, jeep, bee, meat, queen, seal, feet, beak

Page 52

1. jeep
2. tea
3. bee
4. seal
5. queen
6. meat
7. weed
8. peas
9. team

Page 53

Check that children have completed all words with the letter *y*.

1. sky; *colored red*
2. happy; *colored green*
3. cry; *colored red*
4. sixty; *colored green*
5. dry; *colored red*
6. puppy; *colored green*
7. fry; *colored red*
8. bunny; *colored green*
9. why; *colored red*

Page 54

1. happy
2. twenty
3. bunny
4. puppy
5. tiny
6. Baby
7. cry
8. sly

Page 55

1. meat
2. tie
3. rain
4. cane
5. fry
6. goat
7. kite
8. cube
9. weed
10. robe
11. plane
12. bay

Page 56

1. Bees are at home in a hive.
2. Jay can play the flute.
3. The baby mule is cute.
4. Dad will try to bake a lime pie.

Page 57

Children should color the following pictures:

a: jay, sail, game
e: queen, seal
i: bike, pie, sky
o: goat, hoe, robe
u: mule, tube, fuse

Page 58

Jean Hits a Home Run

Page 59

Children should color the following pictures:

barn, harp, star, shark, dart, yarn, arm, jar

Page 60

Children should write the letters *ar* under the following pictures:

1. ar 4. ar 7. ar 12. ar
2. ar 6. ar 10. ar

Page 61

Children should color the following pictures:

stork, thorn, fort, torch, fork, porch

Page 62

Children should write the letters *or* under the following pictures:

1. or 4. or 7. or 10. or
3. or 6. or 8. or 12. or

Page 63

1. purse
2. twirl
3. fern
4. girl
5. stir
6. surf
7. skirt
8. nurse
9. shirt

Page 64

1. fur
2. fern
3. letter
4. purse
5. burns
6. herd
7. circle
8. bird

Page 65

1. surf
2. fork
3. shirt
4. girl
5. herd
6. barn
7. car
8. fern
9. bird
10. horn
11. scarf
12. church

Page 66

1. Circle: barn, church, park, fort, yard
2. Circle: stork, shark, horse, bird
3. Circle: horn, snarl, organ, harp, chirp, purr, snort
4. Circle: barn, horse, corn, dirt, herd
5. Circle: spur, shorts, scarf, shirt, skirt

Page 67

horn

Page 69

1. o
2. y
3. u_e
4. ar
5. a
6. oa
7. or
8. o_e
9. a_e
10. u
11. ee
12. ir

Page 70
1. fly
2. trip
3. meet
4. pack
5. take
6. puppy
7. six
8. sky
9. stars
10. bird
11. peel
12. pie

Page 71
1. *a*
2. *i*
3. *e*
4. *er*
5. *oo*
6. *y*
7. *u*
8. *a*
9. *i_e*
10. *u*
11. *o_e*
12. *oy*

Page 72
1. grow
2. home
3. seeds
4. dirt
5. need
6. use
7. day
8. side
9. buy
10. fern
11. green
12. fine

Page 73
1. *sk*   4. *sm*   7. *sl*
2. *sn*   5. *sk*   8. *sn*
3. *st*   6. *sl*   9. *st*

Page 74
1. *sp*   4. *sw*   7. *tw*
2. *tw*   5. *sp*   8. *sp* or *st*
3. *sc*   6. *tw*   9. *sc*

Page 75
1. smile
2. star
3. twins
4. twig
5. snake
6. skunk
7. twenty
8. stamp
9. scale
10. slide
11. spoon
12. swing

Page 76
1. *str*   4. *scr*   7. *str*
2. *spr*   5. *spl*   8. *scr*
3. *str*   6. *str*   9. *spr*

Page 77
1. sky
2. stars
3. sparkle
4. screen
5. twirl
6. strong
7. smoke
8. swing

Page 78
1. Mom sprays paint on the screen.
2. We like to skate in the city square.
3. The skunk smells a rose.
4. The snowman is wearing Dad's scarf.

Page 79
1. *fr*   4. *br*   7. *dr*
2. *cr*   5. *dr*   8. *cr*
3. *br*   6. *cr*   9. *fr*

Page 80
1. *gr*   4. *cr*   7. *pr*
2. *tr*   5. *tr*   8. *gr*
3. *pr*   6. *gr*   9. *tr*

Page 81
1. grapes
2. brick
3. prize
4. crab
5. drum
6. train
7. frame
8. grill
9. crib
10. drill
11. fruit
12. truck

Page 82
1. drive
2. truck
3. bricks
4. fruit
5. brake
6. bridge
7. try
8. crash

Page 83
1. *cl*   4. *fl*   7. *bl*
2. *fl*   5. *cl*   8. *pl*
3. *gl*   6. *gl*   9. *cl*

Page 84
1. blocks
2. flag
3. clock
4. glass
5. flip
6. clap
7. plane
8. flute
9. clown
10. plum
11. black
12. globe

Page 85
1. plum
2. flag
3. clown
4. plane
5. globe
6. glass
7. fly
8. clock

Page 86
1. clown
2. clucks
3. flaps
4. plays
5. glass
6. plate
7. plant
8. clap

Page 87
1. *br*   5. *fl*   9. *spl*   13. *tr*
2. *cr*   6. *tw*   10. *fr*   14. *spr*
3. *sp*   7. *dr*   11. *pl*   15. *sl*
4. *str*   8. *sm*   12. *tw*

Page 88
1. string
2. branch
3. glass
4. sled
5. strong
6. twig
7. snow
8. smell

Page 89

Page 90
1. Steve scored the prize goal.
2. Chris grows big green plants.
3. The baby in the crib is crabby.
4. Cleo brushes and braids her hair.

Page 91
1. *nt*   4. *nd*   7. *nt*
2. *mp*   5. *nt*   8. *sp*
3. *st*   6. *st*   9. *sk*

Page 92
1. wrist
2. plant
3. stamp
4. dent
5. jump
6. tent
7. desk
8. band
9. stump
10. nest
11. wasp
12. mask

Page 93
1. bank
2. stamp
3. breakfast
4. west
5. vest
6. damp
7. stump
8. fast

Page 94
1. Jan has on the best mask.
2. Mr. Rusk takes the stump off the land.
3. The class gives the band a hand.
4. The ants crawl into the plant.

Page 95
1. *mp*   4. *nd*   7. *sk*   10. *nt*
2. *sp*   5. *st*   8. *nt*   11. *sp*
3. *st*   6. *nd*   9. *mp*   12. *sk*

Page 96
1. jump
2. fast
3. test
4. best
5. stand
6. rest
7. past
8. champ

Page 97
1. went, west, vest, vent, dent
2. disk, dusk, tusk, task, tank
3. land, lend, bend, bent, cent

Page 99

1. *fr* 4. *sn* 7. *dr* 10. *mp*
2. *nt* 5. *cl* 8. *cr* 11. *nd*
3. *sk* 6. *tw* 9. *sk* 12. *mp*

Page 100

1. hint
2. trees
3. plums
4. brown
5. clear
6. cold
7. sky
8. squirrels
9. nest
10. grass
11. twigs
12. sweater

Page 101

1. *cr* 4. *sl* 7. *tr* 10. *nt*
2. *gr* 5. *str* 8. *sl* 11. *st*
3. *nd* 6. *br* 9. *sw* 12. *nt*

Page 102

1. frog
2. swam
3. jump
4. fly
5. wind
6. Flip
7. cry
8. pond
9. raft
10. rest
11. splash
12. glide

Page 103

1. *ch* 4. *wh* 7. *ch*
2. *ch* 5. *ch* 8. *wh*
3. *wh* 6. *wh* 9. *ch*

Page 104

1. *sh* 4. *th* 7. *sh*
2. *th* 5. *sh* 8. *th*
3. *sh* 6. *sh* 9. *th*

Page 105

1. shore
2. shells
3. sharks
4. whales
5. thorns
6. them
7. shy
8. When

Page 106

1. sheep
2. chick
3. thorn
4. chair
5. whale
6. shirt
7. cheese
8. shark
9. wheat
10. thumb
11. them
12. wheel

Page 107

1. child
2. shine
3. wheel
4. phone
5. shoes
6. whip
7. chair
8. think

Page 108

1. *ch* 4. *ch* 7. *th*
2. *ch* 5. *th* 8. *ch*
3. *th* 6. *ch* 9. *ch*

Page 109

1. *tch* 4. *sh* 7. *ck*
2. *sh* 5. *tch* 8. *tch*
3. *ck* 6. *ck* 9. *sh*

Page 110

1. *nk* 4. *ng* 7. *nk*
2. *nk* 5. *nk* 8. *nk*
3. *ng* 6. *nk* 9. *ng*

Page 111

1. ring
2. cloth
3. bench
4. tooth
5. skunk
6. hatch
7. duck
8. fish
9. watch
10. sock
11. porch
12. trunk

Page 112

1. ranch
2. watch
3. patch
4. brush
5. porch
6. fish
7. ring
8. bunk

Page 113

1. *kn* 4. *kn* 7. *kn*
2. *kn* 5. *kn* 8. *wr*
3. *wr* 6. *kn* 9. *wr*

Page 114

1. knot
2. wreck
3. wrist
4. knee
5. knit
6. write
7. wrench
8. knight
9. knock
10. knife
11. wreath
12. wren

Page 115

1. patch
2. chick
3. knock
4. think
5. splash
6. wrench
7. them
8. whale

Page 117

1. *ch* 4. *kn* 7. *kn* 10. *ck*
2. *wr* 5. *nk* 8. *th* 11. *ng*
3. *tch* 6. *wr* 9. *sh* 12. *kn*

Page 118

1. ranch
2. long
3. white
4. flock
5. fish
6. path
7. thorns
8. cheese
9. them
10. skunk
11. bath
12. think

Page 119

1. wrench
2. ship
3. bath
4. thumb
5. chick
6. shirt
7. bench
8. wheel
9. catch
10. whip
11. chart
12. moth

Page 120

1. sing
2. cheese
3. lunch
4. each
5. wren
6. fish
7. dish
8. knee
9. brush
10. think
11. much
12. wish

Answer Key
Core Skills Phonics, Grade 2